HERE ON RUE MORGUE AVENUE

HYSTERICAL BOOKS

HERE ON RUE MORGUE AVENUE

CYNIE CORY

HYSTERICAL BOOKS

TALLAHASSEE, FLORIDA 2018

Cover Image: Jeff Distefano   jeffdistefano.com
Cover Design: Esther Lee
Design, production: Jay Snodgrass
Type Styles: body text in Bodoni URW and titles in Aktiv
Grotesk

Library of Congress Cataloging-in-Publication Data
House of Rue Morgue Avenue — First Edition
ISBN — 978-0-940821-07-1
Library of Congress Cataloging Card Number —
2018931735

HYSTERICAL BOOKS
1506 Wekewa Nene
Tallahassee, Florida 32301
Website: www.hystericalbooks.com
mail: hystericalbooks@gmail.com
Published in the United States by

Hysterical Books
First Edition, 2018

Acknowledgements

Some of these poems have previously appeared in the following magazines, to whose editors, grateful acknowledgement is made:

Barrow Street: "Somewhere in There"

Court Green: "The King's Highway"

Diner: "End Song," "Mercy Island," "Ransom"

Green Mountains: "No Deserter, No Deserter," "Suicide
                        Park," "What Was It You Wanted?"

Gulf Stream: "Hopperesque"

Hotel Amerika: "Petrarch at Least," "Walt Whitman Sleeps

La Fovea: "Cadaver," "Carbonator Blues in B-Flat,"
                        "Exile," "Go Melt Back Into the Night"

La Petite Zine: "Art for Art's Sake," "Boat," "Chronic,"
                        "There Are Illuminated Signs Throughout
                        This Flight," "Pornographic"

Mid-American Review: "Gee, My Life's a Funny Thing"

Passages North: "Do You Want to Take My Picture?"
                        "Robbery"

Rhino: "I Can't Stay In Here," "I Can't Stay In
                        Here, Ain't It Clear?"

Shade: "Apocryphal Blues," "Fall the Fall," "Marxist Theory Provided"

I wish to acknowledge Lord George Byron's epic poem, "Childe Harold's Pilgrimage" which inspired the narrative of these songs.

I am indebted to Denis Johnson, the great American poet and writer, whose eponymous young hero of his early novel *Fiskadoro*, will not let me go.

Thanks to David Dodd Lee who enthusiastically embraced these poems from the start, and who told me to buy the guitar.

A solid to Brenda Rabelais, who helped me walk through a heavy grief for a heavy long time.

Thank you especially to renaissance man Jay Snodgrass, my twin brother, who generously published this manuscript and who understands icebergs.

To those who came before me

to the memory of

Philip Stevens Pearce

September 28, 1953 - January 3, 2018

Contents

HERE ON RUE MORGUE AVENUE

But where is he, the Pilgrim of my song,
The being who upheld it through the past?
                              ~Byron

                         *

Passion or feeling, purpose, grief or zeal,–
Which is the tyrant spirit of our thought,
Is a stern task of soul...

                              ~Byron

                         *

And I'll tell it and think it and speak it and breathe it
And reflect it from the mountain so all souls can see it
Then I'll stand on the ocean until I start sinkin'
But I'll know my song well before I start singin'
                              ~Dylan

                         *

Because something is happening here
But you don't know what it is
Do you, Mister Jones?

                              ~Dylan

And from his native land resolved to go . . .

~ Byron

Boat

There's a way to see the no from here scrapes
dawn behind a pomegranate. Iced, stoned
the sky is barbed nostalgic hushed bone shapes
to the west of us shimmers the new formed
allegiance. Imaginary distance
swan song parable blue-print done. Bury

the rudder under the lover, one glance
escapes from shore — A lonely row — to France.

There are Illuminated Signs throughout this Flight

If there's terror in the sky I want you
in it. Could be the doormat, or headset —
Government of lies invades our minds — Proof
means nothing. But fear, ah. What residence
of mice takes my tongue, my brain, my gland?
Let's reroute the theatre that hovers

over no land. The intelligence bland
as a cocktail watered down in demand.

Chronic

The mind's a prison, the heart's unlocked clucks
time, holds luck out for ransom like an orange.
But I know it's the war of love that plucks
men's eyes. Sad ride. Handsome pride in the morgue
you never see. I myself am lacked, lost,
curbed to the parameter of nothing.

A cosmonaut semi-conducted, caught
without freefall, force of zero, unsought.

Crash on the levee, mama
Swamp gonna rise
No boats gonna row
~Dylan

The T.V. crew was there to film it, they jumped right over me,
Later on that evening, I watched it on T.V.
~Dylan

Pornographic

No wind. Just the tick of dark. The smart bomb
without a closet. Republic of hype,
I'm awake all night. Nothing news. So long
American character, complete wipe-
out. In my little room I am a page
of nothing. As winter I see that snow

is chloroform but I know the storm. Wage
no resistance, sleep inside the grenade.

Art for Art's Sake

Who said hack up her body? Who dared? Mir-
ror lodged in the hand. Who hacked her up? One
Istanbul from Constantinople — Sheer
words will take your luck. The road blocks are none
of your business. Like a hootenanny
without a buzz. This indecision's bug-

gin' me. I stand for chance in the way free-
dom fighters wreck their planes. We lose for grief.

Your Best Violence

The jury's a murdered whore, who's listening?
I'm the core of no one's story. Crypt on
time. Buried dog I loved all along, cling
to lonely. And you! Throaty ruin long
enduring — Let's just dance against the black.
Tomorrow is a resume, a prop-

er slap, the skull in hand the one scratched track
snow won't cover. Ten thousand miles of past.

And grief with grief continuing still to blend
                    ~Byron

Machinery of Dust

You know the dichotomy: mind and heart.
Every day prison. What stops the mind's words?
I'm rocked. A hemorrhage told me stones the cart
won't pull. Same kaleidoscope of tourists.
Red flame jerks inside the bone-cave of home.
Body, spend it. Rent it out to sea, chuck

the broken order to the dogs that foam
and run free as this beast in me I own.

Capitalist Down

I saw the fog split the sky like a thor-
oughfare on fire. The agency tricked
me, disappeared pilot at sea over
the edge of America addicted
to my ancestors, transmitter like gum
popping my eardrums. We were meant to work

weren't we? Proletariat angel, hum
the pinnacled dawn to zero. Time's come.

This is No Factory

On the way to the amphitheatre
the amputee won. The turnstiles hummed
a misdemeanor, would not create her.
Midsummer snow permeated the drummed
difference. Around us helicopters rose.
Without us, love had everything — The end

of Jacqueline Onassis, I suppose.
We pinned silence to the wall and we broke.

I've been ten thousand miles in the mouth of a graveyard
~Dylan

The sky is on fire
And I must go.
~Dylan

Welcome to the Socialist Party

The city rests against my hip like prop-
aganda. I can't do it. Let it shift
a foreward door. Septimus could not stop
his mind from panting. It's tough to live blis-
tered and falling. Like swallowing the sea
in folly. There's always a future horse

chained and bridled. To be a rider, me!
In the midnight glare of apology.

The Last Sleep

Distance shoves white into the white mind white.
Murdered door, the bridge of furthermore burns
white. A sky packed tight with hindsight, polite
curvature, wide blinding-point overturns
white. Meeting place of white and white. What cage
is true — resilient and criminal, force-

count time — North? Hurry, courage is the stage
of the mind without a verse iced in blades.

The Language of Another America

The matinee's split in two, desire's
on the barge. Verge of nothing, rock of stage
left – pickled grief, punk forgiveness, wire's
final fray. Into the mother mouth, page
after page, cinematic scream — lanced dream —
Can't you see? I am not the America

I wanted to be. Scissor me. The queen
of verbal fecundities renders me.

Amputee's Devotion

If you wanted me as far as Nova
Scotia you'd never see the sun. Birches
silver toothed against the above. Love a
core element of derision lurches
for the breeze. You could have helped me
believe in something. My vagabond mind

poised for apocalypse, guillotine speed
of your burial, no sutures no scream.

The Hamlet Test

Filth. Ghost in the hall — rips the night from earth.
Erstwhile feet that own no shoes. Earnest dawn,
that hurried song. It hurts to butcher worth.
You don't know. What dragon's hope? It's all wrong.
What good is luck? God's done. Can't kill this ner-
vous tongue. Gutted night. Sealed ice. The mind clicks

a hollow tune. Pornographic blue. Swerves
all over you. The rest beyond is words.

Better jump down a manhole
Light yourself a candle
                    ~Dylan

Skeleton Keys in the Rain

There's no way out of here, soul says to mind.
Inside the grand disable, everything
is exile. It all returns sometime.
Look how the future will not stop ringing
under me. There's a bird I swear I saw
rise inside the dirt erupting across

the sky like an electric pale guitar.
What it takes to be so far, lovely star.

Hopperesque

Locked in France. No skull about it, berries
on the lips of the girl who wants it — blue
all over you, avenues light worries
like a house in a field. You crouch to move
without a sonnet. There is no forest
bare and equal as the Florida sun.

When you arrive, you're done. The way the west
exists: In a coal mine a canary's nest.

We're Surrounded

Shock to wreck the templed night to prove right
around the cornered sleeve, collapse and grieve
—: Luck is the jury that never meets, Christ
don't waste a blink. The blistered mind's asleep.
Constitution in the gutter, the truth
a worried wall. The sky is framed, pummels

the brain dead on. Confess nothing, you lose
the right to remain. It's Kafka cruel.

Turn and Face the Strange

There's a war in you. 1942.
Guitar with broken string. Somehow it rains.
We're all in chains. It's cruel the way you tune
the range of your vermilion rage — Takes brains
not money to rise above the self — Gunned
into a bunker that's home, another

country you moan, half-split, redundant, stunned,
anonymous, promiseless — ill-tongued.

Apothecary

Is your head a rifle? A trifle
underpaid? I adore you, unafraid
to wallow in my horticultural
vial. Into my suffering brigade
of one I dip. Any less dangerous
an interior split. — O rose thorny

in the wind-torn house be sure, serious
as a motorcade that is poised in loss.

Somewhere in There

I've watched the coffee cup drop from my hand
and not even seen it — That sub tropic
part of me now philanthropic hard-band
metaphorically corked. I'm electric
without a transmit — The union is lost!
Flag machine asleep at the window. Phone

the notary public, it's beef! O cost
you cannibal, you blinking holocaust.

Love Minus Zero

I know the stage, we all behave badly.
But I'm better friends with Jackson Pollock
than with Divinci, understandably.
As an infant I suffered from colic
and was told to stop it. Love that made worms
out of meat. If I place my frostbitten

hand against your heart, will I sleep in urns
that divide me? Don't describe me. Love burns.

Hart Crane, Too

The phone cord around my neck like a charm
can't be beat. Why not me? I'm serious
it's freezing. Oh, confess. I saw alarm
in your eyes the night you died. A theory's
an enemy this stage — The broken play's
a machine that won't stop. Words fall to dust.

The hardwood heart is scraped up. It's the place
where I leave breaking all that breaking breaks.

China, Maybe

Is there an island in the mind that I
can get to? There's a rock inside my gut
you won't believe it, that I love you — Try
to visit anywhere I dare you. Luck
shapes us into rivers I'm sorry I'm past
monuments past factories past the way

we never came. It's all the same — You laugh.
I can't there's something ridiculous halved.

Emily Dickinson Rage

In the hair of a target-split who wins?
Who built this city? I'll burn it, destroy
your shoes, your car, your bed. What dream expends
this much soul? Bloody dog inside a joy
for nothing. The will is always the way
around the corner, through the door — the morgue

of the eponymous mistress. Don't say
life is a gun — I want the world delay.

Rain on Old Compton Street

There's the reap you hoe. Opportunity
a drawing on your back. I'll last the last
resentment, upstaged by idiocy.
Slain days we can't retrieve or change — gassed
planet rimmed by no light. My love, I've come
here to chip the distance back to blue, not

because I hate but because I love. Rush!
Look inside the ice of your mind and trust.

Tell me great hero, but please make it brief
Is there a hole for me to get sick in?
                                             ~Dylan

It's all been designed," he said, "to make you lose your mind,
And when you go back to find it, there's nothing there to find.
                                             ~Dylan

Chaplinesque

— Just a beginning, all of us faking
 it prematurely, here with my stutter-
 step like I'm building an igloo, raking
 the snow from ice. My tongue to her shudder
 became a paradisiacal flow-
 er, the odor of sea washed over us

words we could not see like a future crawl-
ing from us cinematic speed I vow.

Suicide Park

She helped me see my wooden sleeves were brit-
tle. I'm no longer astonished by cost —
I earned the losses of my brilliant dish —
Pluck the bones of this. Establish the raw
annihilation, you beautiful Queen.
I'm on the heath looking for Emma Thomp-

son. If I weren't awake I'd go to sleep.
How easy to break the habit of being.

I Can't Stay in Here

There is a country where all this matters.
End of home, winter inside winter. Locked
island, glassed-in song. Clink to stone and hearse.
We walk into the glittery sea wrenched
incomplete. Granite slabs lap in sun-sick
scabs. I don't care what you say I'm black-stench

grief. Throw a brick it won't break. I'm a tick
in the lip of Louis Armstrong's face. Br-r-ip.

To the Republic

This is my exile. Snow drifts to waist.
God Land. God Money in a hell frozen
white white sleep. I have traveled star-laced, chased
the dark miles of loneliness, driven.
I was to enter a language that helped
no one. (Take this down in secret writing.)

Dog to a bone, unbury me. Corrupt
union of hypocrisy, I once knelt.

Some Philosophy

It was sturdy, the way we wept past June —
No reply. I think I'll lie on the South
Bank, cleave my tongue, it's true. There's ample proof
we need a coup. Drop the world and house
ourselves in comedy. Break our minds back
to the majority. The election

was the people's authority hijacked.
In sooth, I love you more than I love fact.

Remove yon skull from out the scatter'd heaps:
Is that a temple where a God may dwell?
                    ~Byron

It's easy to see without looking too far
That not much
Is really sacred.
                    ~Dylan

She's Nothing Like You

Rip the Jew in two. Put her in anoth-
er country. She's carbonic in her pose.
No one knows, not her — She's buried a love
of snow, a granite coast. Inside her rose
nothing ambiguous. I knew her pressed
against the syllogist like a guitar

unplayed, held her body in rain possessed,
no less. Her hyperintelligence X'd.

Good Thing it's America

Half whole she rips me to the door. Know her,
the over-crafted war, tight shade. Rain hard-
ens then breaks. About to say what's lower
than grief? The wrench of me won't pry apart
the core invader, defibulator.
I am a percolator in a black

and white colored classic movie. Greater
than grinds I last as a way to take her.

Empty Dream Full/Full Dream Empty

Shut my eyes to the dark, explode every-
thing I know. The heart attacks like a miser
in the end, sized and shadowed. M. Bovary
mattered. Crafted madness swim, the lobster
is your advocate. Charmed and slow, royal
infinity's a rogue you want to hang

with. Lover of two, master of fuck all
words, the living hearse — we're all so fragile.

Rogue State

Intelligence the pharmaceutical
zero army of gone. A new improved
aphrodisiac killer. O fragile
mathematical pawn, unearn the unglued
frame. Brave idea, that cannabis (plus
the inside of a shoe.) They swallow rights

for you, Jew-sailor-Christian-monger — Nuts.
John Wilkes Booth, you know how soft the skull dusts.

These Cats is Killing Themselves

What is my country if it's not myself?
To read the wind I have no flag. This map
like nothing real. Some nights another shell.
You can count on what we've known for years, Mac.
No one memorizes its tenants like
a veil. The war keeps trying. Inside west

is right, the popular throat is a white
obscenity. Take a bite. It's just right.

Exile

Out here I manage to sing, what a boat
I am. The unspiritual God decides
in stenotype there's no compromise, dope
to the left of me rehearsing rain chides,
me a hollow cost. Wooden army lost
at sea. Telepathy, antipathy.

What'll it be ma cherie? The star-cross'd
troubador's a bore. Which way forth? I'm sloshed.

At Your Own Chosen Speed

I ask what city. A way to invent
a stall. Everything's a falling tower,
wrong and beautiful. Hopeless hours spent
in glass. The saddled past a smashed flower.
How I've wanted to last beyond the talk.
You're a shifting river's current reversed.

We need an engineer, a lonely God.
In a dark like this your body is lost.

Robbery

It was like I'd never been to New York.
The tall buildings were pummeled by snowfall.
Ambulances were everywhere ignored.
I wanted investigation, equal
resuscitation. Cavities searched and named, an Arch
Bishop who'd known my mother in a dream.

There she was, where I could not see her search
for me. Strange planet this Manhattan. Hurts.

These Cats is Killing Themselves

What is my country if it's not myself?
To read the wind I have no flag [this map
like nothing real some nights (another shell
you can count on) what we've known for years: shrap-
nel memorizing its tenant, a veil
able but the war likes trying)] inside

the west. The heat is a kingdom for frail
obscenities. Telling us nothing fails.

Were She World

The voice gone, philosophy still listening.
Formica breaks the sun without trying
to move me. Contemptible body, thing
of remember. How would you know widening
above you the universe? Some say time
contracted then took you through it, outside

now. Thinking doesn't help, it will not find
you. When I form your name you're in my mind.

Sonnet

By what name? Planetary haze, lend me
a view. Jack up the state that I am in.
The love poem is no accident. The tree
in me is a soliloquy. Open
the moment, the sentimental grip. Hey
Charlotte Smith! In this dark wedge, in debtor's

debt, I place a bowl cracked and glued, and face
the moon-chained terror of the soul's escape.

And they laid him down on the jailhouse ground
With an iron chain around his neck.
                    - Dylan

Summer Dissolve

Time is a nevermind, a hollow eye,
a stone against a mirror — What are you fear?
There's no bridge to get to her still I try
outside Raphael's framed martyr the weird
light of sky commits itself to something
in me — the region I seek to mend, her

eponymous grin like nostalgia's wing
deletes the accordion sea I sing.

Exploratory Surgery

Here you are a wooden heart. That's a start,
summer of sciences. Help me finish
my sentences. Theory of swarm, a cart
with me in it, bartered. Diminish
me. Who decides to leave against the green
intelligence? The soul grinds. Requires

a new form. Dislodge the bilious spleen.
The mind is an after-lock of being.

Ingest This

Coming is the text of you though it's not
very close. Pluck the tea bag from the cup.
I'm a ghost. What else maroons your head? Walk
through it. To the window: We didn't fuck.
Lapsang Souchong rubs my tongue. Listen I
never listen — Hyphens burn on the limbs

of trees. Hysteria is breached. Why
an Anglican sun predicates the sky.

Cocktail Blues

This kind of heat consumes the right to rise.
Shove it into drive, brutalize the noon.
It's hard to say aloud (pilgrim proud) — Try
to understand when the sky hits us soon
it's not over. Carborator, alter-
nator, wind-gush, fumes. It's up to you am-

bivalence, I love your manly hands or
is it circumstance that splits into war?

Banishment, Banishment

I married America, it was con-
tractual. They said it would kill me ice
down if I searched beyond the armored dawn.
Was I not once an immigrant? Exile
of England? Mother, mother, daughter cling
to the transitory I. Fields of rye.

Who stole Walt Whitman and Hart Crane? I drink
eight reasons why I should leave for nothing.

September 7, 2004

I know the borderland, mind divided
by rhyme, tin can concrete scraped, dented page,
forced escape, vulnerable stranger widened
like a western sky wrecked in blue, the age
of America lassoed. Theatrical
you. Vertical and deserted. I'm through

weathering my days with the practical.
You come to me phantasmagorical.

How to Survive the Longest War

I don't remember this fret-by-fret, keyed
to run, o sentimental gun in mouth.
It took a couch, a skin of teeth to bleed
the crippled demon from this mortared house.
There was the plastic dream in shreds, stuck roars
that blacked the sun, and streets that ripped apart

the mind — blocks of ice. An igloo knows north
blank as love. The threat of home toward, untoward.

. . . my soul wanders; I demand it back
~ Byron

Bury Me

I give I gave I mock the wall I walk
like Icarus brave and referential,
glass words locked. I look in the face of loss.
The luck of me's a bone insubstantial.
The dogs they lick they wag a grave digger
down to the shovel's broken tip. There's wit

inside the grit, always is, I figure.
Out of here is to disappear, sister.

Fall the Fall

A deep depression's setting right across
us like a new intelligence — Give me
another horse! Subdued, unarmed, I brought
a burning book to your embassy,
remarkably. Self-importance is good
enough as evil, the knowledge swift

as a greasy heart without a chest, look!
My brain's higher, wired in advance. Pluck.

Cadaver

dog, Delmore's over here. An icicle
drowning in the dust. I apologize
for the noise inside the skull, miracle
we found him at all. Apollo eyes wide
open. I cry in the elevator
against the mirror. Don't wag your tail, Rip,

you're not the undertaker. O Delmore,
what a fuck in the ass. This evermore.

Forward Song

There is no Ariel, no view to speed
out of muscle — Thigh high this mud storm curse.
Nothing here is plausible. Man, excrete
distance from what's complete. I'm finished. Blur
the windshield with grief. There is no Laura
Brown in me. Lonely as a crown, unsound

ground — Burbage, verbiage, existential ah
ha — The rest is predestiny, voila!

Ode to Yellow

Thin film spittle to flesh. Under your eye
a weaving. I can't get there. I'm all blue
under white. Silver thread, leash of my crimes.
Let's look at it: We're over here: the room
is an advertisement, hearse. Acrobats
harness themselves to a word in the wall.

I can't enjoy it, it's perverse your last
turn on over my head. The slit is bashed.

Tut-Tut

clucked the tongue goodbye. The mind's a matchstick
on the run. I made her come, wild sheer
luck of it. O Father of Lights I'm sick
and blind with it. The shape of rhyme cracked here.
True dawn ripped open, absolute night un-
sleeved. The heart is wide as a carnival

that left while we slept. Permanent question.
Cataract of song, igloo motion.

Carbonator Blues in B-Flat

— There anybody here? I'm not that kind
to disturb a bird I pulled a message
from the earth. Alert said the hurting mind
or the Jew in the colon rhymed send love
send love until the fire died. In sooth
she left no mortal coil, no transist-

or summer wreath disabled lonesome root
a harp spun upside right rusted plinged spoof.

Le Chagrin et la Pitie

The moon's on my lap like a pack of dogs.
London's the pallbearer. America, you won.
Inside the downbeat is (repeat) the lost
idea. Pull your skullcap back, it's done.
The bleeding head in June murmurs France.
What catastrophe deserves another

broken armor? I cannot last this dance
homeward like a truant under street lamps.

Reactor Tractor

I want the roof, no sky louder than dogs.
I can't say what caused it, an atomic
split.   God's silhouette disappeared now lost.
Utilitarian and exotic
is a pack of matches from Harrod's. Blake
told us what the Tyger was but no one

listened. Without vision winter's in place.
The invasion by the United States.

Point of Origin

Who's the warrior? Not me. This train's stop-
ping like a holiday. I'm searched for words
I never had. A backwards plan to plot
what's left. The monkey in my chest disturbs
the nervous sun that spreads across the west-
ern sea. Think of three days it takes to die.

Smeared out landscape — crippled tongue. Fact is dressed
in white. Horizontal mind my palace.

Go Melt Back into the Night

I remember you there against the glare
of my incarceration. Naked bulb,
atomic bomb. In this elsewhere prayer,
you were gone. It was the beginning skulled
to the branches of trees. Poor Hamlet's numb.
Sings a wild tune then hums I'm a blade

in the rest of white. Where were you, Fo-Fum?
I carried a hound dog, a pound of crumbs.

Apocryphal Blues

Unearthed, am I a chronic veteran spent
roadside, glimmering night-tide wind-swept ice
overform, ill-effect, percussive sweat
— idiot balance, overtured chaos,
left wing branched out white failure, tugged in blue?
I remember the view, so orange ago —

freight train winding up my shoe like a move
without forgiveness. What of it? I'm stewed.

I Can't Stay in Here

There is a country where all this matters.
End of home. Winter inside winter. Locked.
I am (nothing) not horse, hearse, kingdom hers,
historic tome, right-train night-train moon cocked
to mind-change, rice-rain, subatomic Christ-
pain, the brain, the brain a sullied wall-blame

the click. We walk the oil slick. It's twice
across the ice before you fall, call, bite.

Draw Bridge

Air splits (who's hanging on?) the mind supine
a verb run-over supreme noetic
shift the surface tic shrugs indifference brine
the after-thought pianistic tryptich
slips the architecture diaphanous.
Here's where I live. (Remember it) Pollock

tried. The space between us lifts as ashes.
The cage door roars chronic vertiginous.

Face Up

Light as object of beauty, precision.
Afterall, what is darkness but three-fourths
an iceberg of the imagination.
That blurry arrangement, a Greek chorus
of stiff goodbyes, porous and muti-
lated. In advance nothing gives, snow press-

es against the chest I'm in, almost dis-
appearing blue, can't move or stop the blizz.

End Song

In this emotional swamp here begins
the cold. No ship on water, no lighthouse
burning light. I pass this way, Finnegan.
It's all up to you. Bird on leaf, edge-mouth
adieu. Oak tree, it can be beautiful
in this one-horse view, can't we make it clean?

What do you mean life? One razor blade dull
with oxides. I knew you, blade of grass. (Bull.)

Her National Razor

The trench we leave behind is you, soldier.
Forget you you say like a freezer-burn, gray-
white theatre, hermetic and trill. Sure
the after-drop bursts the sockets, insane
criminal of adjustment. The private
mind we don't recognize. From the couch, smear

the mute decision. What use armament?
Round the throat daylight hits. I'm Ann Boleyn.

Leave your stepping stones behind, something calls for you.
Forget the dead you've left, they will not follow you
~Dylan

Look out kid
You're gonna get hit
~Dylan

It's Behind You, Look

It was meant to be glorious it rang
from the sky like a thousand murders more
than any other war. Trenchless arrange-
ment, what suffering! In the stable door
we vote rancid. Substantial evidence.
What matters is the horse, methinks. I am

a dancer stuck in motion headed hence
for the floor in measure   silhouetted.

Asleep for the Duration

Silver burn, the common why swept under
the residual table. American
Legion, what's left of the view? Soft prankster,
wooden sky planked by what's behind Wittgen-
stein, linguistic crime. The mind beats itself
with the letter A — It's too far, this change

in our pockets. The current foreign shelf
slips the arbitrary body of wealth.

Western Unwritten

I can't describe it. The pressure of want-
ing to be. Requirement of now. In-
ner sanctions arrive at zero. Flaunt
the burrowed name. Volatile cactus rim,
incinerator noose. Give me a noun,
another way to ride away, to say.

Stranger, in this field of distance, sink sound
into the borrowed armor of the found.

You lose yourself, you reappear
You suddenly find you got nothing to fear
Alone you stand with nobody near
                    ~Bob Dylan

Was it for this you took your sudden journey?
                    ~Byron

Scrap Metal

There it was. Forgotten like a soldier.
We didn't lie. Like half a past she moved
in me without a chance. To last, measure
predominance in a glass, smash it rude.
I'm not here. Now that I'm invisible.
The past is lanced and cloroxed to a scream.

It's been a dream this distance durable
as a manufactured road. Unpassable.

Deconstruction Site

What's left is a phony dressage. A kind
of terror relinquished, understated.
Swarthy and taciturn we turn a timed
religion. Back to back, unrelated
a voice blued to the interior, low
bridge underdeveloped, inferior.

The heart is a crane, immovable crow.
Connection, heavy contradiction, home.

Every Day is Dangerous

As if elegance could get you somewhere
valuable. I thought you were valuable.
Thought you might stick around the thoroughfare.
As if I didn't know — disposable
as an enzyme — you were disappearing.
Everyone's corrupt is what you'd say, well

I don't think so. We're particles smearing
like the sun against the wind. Darjeeling?

Yonder stands your orphan with his gun
Crying like a fire in the sun
~ Dylan

There's a black Mercedes rollin' through the combat zone
Your servants are half dead; you're down to the bone
~ Dylan

Did he not this for France?
~ Byron

From My Back Pages

Who wants to hear about the tide? It's low
or folding back. I see the river rocks
bone-shell sand from the bank where I stand; blow
by blow — comedy of serious thoughts.
The world is living, I forgot! I'll wait
for you in verbal blue precision-spent

on another coast — Hyperion angst,
recall the fractured eye erased, blank,

I Can't Stay in Here, Ain't it Clear?

End of home, winter inside winter locked
island, constituent of nothing first
before us the furnace spreads out the lost
body. A view of what caught the flames thirsts
for relevance. They stole her eloquence,
her herness — everything, all. Blue nothing,

universe dimming to bone tooth sequence
to no journey. (Gone) (God) (Eclipse of) sent.

The Hamlet Letter

Fortinbras, the power of my mild
utopia's safely gone. Go to her.
Go. Say I'm deeply guarded in bile.
I'll manage the rest. The severance a cur-
tain. In two hours I'll go forth to ease
this troubled blood. Award me nothing, love

won't cure me. Invisible by degrees,
I wear Ophelia on my open sleeve.

What's so Renaissance?

Cling to the familiar smacked moon up far
as you can hurl it. Discuss the curve, dis-
connect the humble tyrant day-glo dark,
inter-continental shark. Serious
remark. I'm blond I'm dead I'm not well read.
Throat it up my asphalt junky, I'm paid

by the hours of my heart-panicked dread.
It's all the same, Ben Johnson. Mind zed.

Zing, the Broken Thing

I can't explain it past dawn a river
swarms my head the body's closing it said.
Artificial land unhomed, struck zither.
It's all I can do in this monument.
Shred the form from view, the heart unthreads, stops.
History's a plot. My mind is caught through

the wires of a barbed fence. What talks talks
like the middle of a dream after thoughts.

Mercy Island

The thought wrecked by the view proves optimis-
tic – I'm stable-bound, stapled to the in-
side of your knees. Kilometer-free. Stripped
roofless, sky-jammed, Van Gogh-crammed, coped wherein
the surface is crumbs, surgical, earnest
as a Dali unrepaired. Two of one

sex, half a dozen performances rest
in a cupboard. It's bound to bore. Get dressed.

Love Minus Zero

I'm zig-zagged, snowed. It's unanimous. Ice
my entrails tight I'm stoned. Here hear the give
beneath the cold about to break us. Christ,
your interior is an anarchist.
Love is a winter like this. What I mean
is I need your wrist. A bomb with a view,

phew! We exist, we exist. Shrapnel clean
and true. Come put your hand in mine and dream.

Mediterranean Blues, Approximately

The heart splits a bloody field but the brain's
a train. You can't buy it like a guitar
or eat it like a gun. Mouth a flame's
private blue. Chokes out of you this winter
fugue, solitary. Snow crushes under.
The brain's democracy amphetamine.

O bridge it! The stars are bullets tender
in the flesh of a surviving murmur.

Middle Country

There is no battle line, the war is done.
Dull answers across the sky famously
slip like a sea coming in. What's begun
begins. — My girl, she takes me honestly.
Where night is nailed to a vacant inn wind
doesn't even know. What field of light swells

upon arrival? What's lost in us ends
a long survival we alone invent.

Transit Station

Is there a region that won't sustain us?
Is this it? Snapdragons in the roda-
dendran. How do you suppose? Can't discuss
the napalm, the palindrome for Lorca —
Shimmering recession, don't expect it
to gain momentum — The inverse is true

always — Like Aphrodite, a ticket
to disappear but live forever split.

Petrarch at Least

Nervous blue attacks the wing. Can't think black
inside the burning window. Winter comes
the way I've seen her wreck the bed, hold back
the dominoes in my head. Hear what hums?
Electric fear. I'm a deer without woods.
Let's make it clear: the room is a razor.

All I want is to stay here, understood?
If love comes in at the eye then we're hooked.

I dreamed I saw St. Augustine,
Alive as you or me,
Tearing through these quarters
In the utmost misery
                    ~Dylan

Do You Want to Take My Picture?

So ends the long experiment, the fat
waves of exaggeration, you liar.
Without scraping you off, the asphalt's bad
enough. It sounds like a placebo mur-
dered us. City of crumb. Existential
bar maid. Body of glove, I've had enough

false intelligence. Finger the thistle.
The monument's a shell, artificial.

Farewell, Angelina

I love her like an orange passed out beyond
intelligence. Past the wrist the endive
says it best. Bitter my heart three person'd
chicory. 1:31 a.m. grind
the four lunged sigh — My lover she's a wreck-
age for a strainer, straight edge silver spooned

invader. White turtle doves escape her. Heck,
I'll sweep the dust, peel back my brains, sob, wretch.

David Copperfield

The air is cellophane, my face slips toward
a cataract. The Cadillac in gold
is memory in a blizzard. I lowered
the membrane, sunk past oblivion cold-
dark, flashlight happenstance, dream infested
overdrive. What's left, dust? Snow banks of rust

ridicule me. Fight the ingested
pilgrim's plight. I am far too invested.

Slalom Course

There should be nothing left. I think there is
nothing left. The significant dark. Cut
sky routine. Everything's a question zipped.
It's in the oversleep I dream the rut
iced-over below zero speed of speech
split hair-pin turn away knee-burn fault line

traverse, perfect earth approximate breach
of incumbent snow, body, soul, unbleach.

Marxist Theory Provided

Mustang fuse — corroborator daughter.
The future is a chair against the wall.
Strip the riddle. You can't get blurred for hur-
rying. It's how you leave a ghost not the crawl-
space. It's so much larger when you're armless
strapped inside the shade of North Begonia.

If you could break your brittle bend, undress
words from flesh, you'd come into love not death.

Magician of Robbery

Money and pain. How does one survive it?
Capsized, I'm looking nowhere for a ride.
This is as good as any subject. Split
nothing, duplex wide. Keep swallowing tide
Manhattan high. Pity so little lost.
My little apricot, tres astonished!

Perverse me, center of nothing brought
down like a massacred carpet. A prop.

The Frame of Everything

I don't believe you. Everything is un-
derway. In Hampstead nothing happened. Stiff
and interrupted, I did not weep. Love
rattles inside the mind, inside the rip
of sky. The universe consumes us. Words,
the story of nothing. Make me see. Scrape

clean this flesh. Beat these bones to dust. Unburd-
en the door in the wind. (The window heard.)

Walt Whitman Sleeps

Who's the murderer here? Find a theory
for your words that ground the zero — blip blap
in the in-between I'm lost and weary.
I've seen a bridge that wasn't a bridge, strapped
to the rising water. It's all over
baby blue — Let's repeat: The war's on time

or is it the pharmacy the lover
minds? Too much to dance we soon discover.

Fiskadoro Revisited

She locks the whole accordion, the plot
of dirt at my feet. According to noon,
there's no more room — She invents wood rot
while I'm nailed to her back. How long is soon?
The lover is a robber, aborted
perfume. What day is it the stars collide?

I don't buy the bard's blue eyes. Purported
love lies. Weep, Sally. The heart's distorted.

No Man's Land

How accidental was the blade? It fell
clean through cartilage and bone. The worried
rain, tropical and bruised, complained like hell.
No dog left to tell about the hurried
day. I lack not exactly hope but fear
fact, the coward's way. The sky's away. Few

Heathcliff's resume. The war is my career.
My death letter pocket holds a mirror. Here.

Chemical School

It branched my mind across my eyes there's no-
thing I can do for you in this inspir-
ation. Deep meditation cracks a loaf
of bread. A fag in bed. I wish her fur-
nace was better kept. After all, dubbed mean,
she's still a beauty queen. Imagine rent

is all we've got. Poppycock, uh? Whose scene
is the after-thought? Blow it up, I mean.

This is Not America

Impossible wide water, foreign war
I am. Between borders slipping under
the turnstile's click of syllables morgued
and bladed like thoughts raked for plunder.
Forehead's ripped a corridor July'd through
a vacant lot. Where is the theatre

that Edward Hopper caught? Genius is cruel
as a newsreel that won't avert the view.

The Mind Up

Allegiance, bendable breaks. So breaks ice.
In the side of contentment there's never
never. Fire across the tired price
of I won't believe. She cannot sever
to leave. She is a swallowed thing. I sing
a shut tomorrow, a purple flower.

The cluttered clock won't hold. I think I'll wring
my hands and tell myself that dead is King.

The King's Highway

A question of silence, indecision,
the mind married to marsh, to glacier, no
God, no petticoats up to the knees, Ken
a former this, that. I would like to go,
she thinks, I am not quite finished. So act
like it's affordable, the war and all

the failed missions. I'd sooner break the pact
of invisible archers than be jacked.

Fiskadoro Last Seen

I wish the glacier in my head. Figure
of drowning. Emphysema hock. Cry doubt.
I married you for nothing. Pedicure
mouth. What see? What me? Impose the last drought,
thermonuclear assault. Winter climbs
over us, snaps shut the lake. Private pain.

I am so sick at heart. Sick. O lover,
box of ashes. I've become another.

Notes:

Welcome to the Socialist Party: Septimus is a young war veteran in Virginia Woolf's <u>Mrs. Dalloway</u>.

The Language of Another America: This title refers to <u>The Language of America</u>, by seventeenth century American Roger Williams.

Skeleton Keys in the Rain: From Bob Dylan's "Visions of Johanna."

We're Surrounded: The title is taken from a Ryan Adams song of the same name. "It's Kafka cruel" is a nod to poet Michael Burkhard.

Turn and Face the Strange: The title is a phrase from "Changes," by David Bowie.

Apothecary: This is the voice of Romeo's father, priest/horticulturist in "Romeo and Juliet."

Love Minus Zero: This canto is for Brenda Rabelais.

Rain on Old Compton Street: Old Compton Street is situated in the heart of Soho, an historically gay district of London.

Chaplinesque: A nod to Hart Crane's poem of the same title.

Suicide Park: The title refers to Hampstead Heath where Keats and other Romantics lived.

I Can't Stay in Here: From Dylan's "Just Like a Woman". In 1969 Louis Armstrong was struck in the mouth by a brick.

To the Republic: The phrases, "God Land," "God Money," "I have traveled star-laced," and "Take this down in secret writing" is from I, Roger Williams by Mary Lee Settle.

Some Philosophy: The South Bank refers to the the river Thames.

Rogue State: "(plus the inside of a shoe.) They swallow rights/for you" refers to Homeland Security.

These Cats is Killing Themselves: "Mac" is Mike McClelland.

Exile: "unspiritual God" is from German poet Georg Trakl. The "star-cross'd/troubadour" is a play on Shakespeare's "star cross'd lovers," Romeo and Juliet.

At Your Own Chosen Speed: The title belongs to Bob Dylan's "It Ain't Me, Babe".

Were She World: This poem is dedicated to the memory of my mother.

Sonnet: Charlotte Smith, early Romantic poet/ novelist. While imprisoned for her husband's debts she wrote and sold sonnets in order to feed her children.

Summer Dissolve: Raphael refers to the Spanish painter.

Ingest This: Lapsang Souchong is a smoky Chinese tea.

Banishment, Banishment: The speaker is Roger Williams during his long, cold winter in exile.

How to Survive the Longest War: The couch refers to Freud.

Bury Me: A jig of a nod to the grave digger scene in "Hamlet".

Roger Williams Dead: The speaker of the cantos is a descendent of Williams.

Fall the Fall: "Give me/another horse!" Spoken by King Richard in the battle of Richmond. From Shakespeare's "King Richard III".

Cadaver: Delmore is poet Delmore Schwartz. Our speaker poses as forensic officer who, along with his dog, discovers the great young poet's body.

Forward Song: Ariel is the sprite from Shakespeare's, "The Tempest". Richard Burbage (1567?-1619) was an actor and associate of the Bard. Laura Brown is a character in the film, "The Hours."

Tut-Tut: "O Father of Lights" is taken from I. Roger Williams.

La Chagrin et la Pitie: "The Sorrow and the Pity." Documentary film (Marcel Ophuls, 1969) about the French Resistance and its collaboration with Nazi Germany during WWII. This poem is dedicated to Sally Karioth.

Reactor Tractor: Harrod's is the London department store. Lines five and six refer to William Blake who wrote the poem, "The Tyger".

Go Melt Back Into the Night: The title is from Dylan's "It Ain't Me, Babe". Hamlet is mad with grief. This poem is for my sweet, darling Flannery.

Gee, My Life's a Funny Thing: From David Bowie's song, "Young American".

I Can't Stay in Here: The title is from Dylan's "Just Like a Woman".

Draw Bridge: Refers to the painter Jackson Pollock.

End Song: Finnegan refers James Joyce's, Finnegan's Wake.

Her National Razor: Term for Guillotine in France. Anne Boleyn was Henry VIII's second wife.

Every Day is Dangerous: The title is taken from Virginia Woolf's, Mrs. Dalloway. Darjeeling is a pleasant, light tea.

From My Back Pages: Is a Dylan song title.

I Can't Stay in Here, Ain't It Clear? From Dylan's "Just Like a Woman".

The Hamlet Letter: A fictional letter. Fortinbras is the Prince of Norway in Shakespeare's "Hamlet".

What's so Renaissance? This poem refers to Ben Johnson, the seventeenth century epigraphist. Zed is the word for zero in Britain.

Mercy Island: England.

Love Minus Zero: The title is taken from Dylan song, "Love Minus Zero/No Limit".

Transit Station: Lorca refeers to the great Spanish poet and playwright who was executed by the Franco government in 1936.

Petrarch at Least: Petrarch is a fourteenth century Italian poet. "Love comes in at the eye" essentially it means "love at first sight" or "romantic love."

Do You Want to Take My Picture?: The title is from a song by the group Filter. "Do you want to take my picture/because I won't remember."

Farewell, Angelina: Another Dylan title. "Bitter my heart three person'd/chicory" is a play on John Donne's Sonnet 14 which begins "Batter my heart three-person'd God; for you.

David Copperfield: The magician.

Marxist Theory Provided: North Begonia is a place the mind knows only in absurdity.

The Frame of Nothing: "I don't believe you" was Dylan's reply to a heckler who had cried out,

"Judas!" during a 1966 Albert Hall concert in London when he had first gone electric.

Fiskadoro: Fiskadoro is Denis Johnson's adolescent protagonist from the novel of the same name. Fiskadoro is one of few survivors of a nuclear war.

No Man's Land: Heathcliff is a character in Bronte's <u>Wuthering Heights</u>.

Chemical School: The word "fag" in line four refers to a cigarette. Here it is tongue-in-cheek.

This is Not America: The title is from a song by David Bowie and Pat Metheny.

The King's Highway: From the English poem of the same name.

Fiskadoro Last Seen: Again, Denis Johnson's young survivor.

ABOUT THE AUTHOR

Cynie Cory is the author of *American Girl* and *Self-Portrait as Fiskadoro's Lover After the End of the World*. She is a graduate of the University of Iowa Writers' Workshop and Florida State University where she took a doctorate in English. Her poems have appeared in many journals and magazines, including *The American Poetry Review*, *Colorado Review*, *New American Writing*, *Ploughshares*, *Triquarterly* and *And Here: 100 Years of Michigan's Upper Peninsula Writing*. Cory is a Michigander from Marquette yet she makes her home in Tallahassee, Florida.

CPSIA information can be obtained
at www.ICGtesting.com
Printed in the USA
FFHW02n1340100818
47708094-51348FF